HOME INSULATION
KNOW-HOW

HOME INSULATION
KNOW-HOW

Mike Lawrence
Consultant Editor: Ian Penberthy

HERMES
HOUSE

This edition is published by Hermes House

Hermes House is an imprint of
Anness Publishing Ltd
Hermes House, 88–89 Blackfriars Road,
London SE1 8HA
tel. 020 7401 2077; fax 020 7633 9499;
info@anness.com

A CIP catalogue record for this book is
available from the British Library.

Publisher: Joanna Lorenz
Managing Editor: Judith Simons
Art Manager: Clare Reynolds
Project Editor: Felicity Forster
Editor: Ian Penberthy
Photographers: Colin Bowling & John Freeman
Designer: Bill Mason
Editorial Reader: Hayley Kerr
Production Controller: Joanna King

Additional text: Diane Carr, Mike Collins,
David Holloway & Brenda Legge

Previously published as Do It Yourself
Home Insulation

10 9 8 7 6 5 4 3 2 1

The author and publishers have made
every effort to ensure that all instructions
contained within this book are accurate
and safe, and cannot accept liability for any
resulting injury, damage or loss to persons
or property, however it may arise. If in any
doubt as to the correct procedure to follow
for any home improvements task, seek
professional advice.

CONTENTS

INTRODUCTION

Insulation is a means of preventing heat from escaping from a house. Heat loss can occur through roofs, walls, floors, doors and windows, and each of these can be insulated in different ways – with loose-fill or blanket insulation, or by installing double glazing, to name a few.

Related to insulation is draughtproofing, which is also a method of reducing heat loss, particularly under doors, through letter plate openings and keyholes, and through gaps in windows.

Insulating and sealing a house totally is not the answer, however, as there always needs to be some air ventilation to prevent condensation, which can lead to mould and structural damage. So a combination of insulation, draughtproofing and ventilation is required.

This book shows how to insulate, draughtproof and ventilate the main areas of the home where heat loss can be a problem. Doing this will save energy and money, and will also cut down on unnecessary wastage of fossil fuels, which in turn causes the widespread environmental problems associated with the release of carbon dioxide into the atmosphere.

CAUSES OF HEAT LOSS

The primary areas of heat loss are through the roof, walls and floors – around 25 per cent of heat is lost through the roof and pipework, 35 per cent through the walls, and 15 per cent through the floors – so these are the first areas to work on.

Doors and windows are the next most likely places where heat is lost, due to draughts coming through gaps and cracks. About 15 per cent of heat loss is attributed to poor draughtproofing.

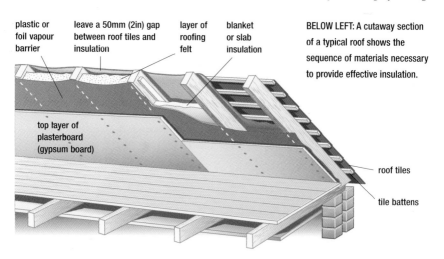

plastic or foil vapour barrier

leave a 50mm (2in) gap between roof tiles and insulation

layer of roofing felt

blanket or slab insulation

top layer of plasterboard (gypsum board)

BELOW LEFT: A cutaway section of a typical roof shows the sequence of materials necessary to provide effective insulation.

roof tiles

tile battens

ABOVE: Draughts can enter your home through the smallest of gaps. You can easily prevent draughts through keyholes by installing keyhole covers.

CAUSES OF CONDENSATION

Condensation can be caused by a lack of ventilation and over-insulation in properties not designed for it, both inside the rooms and within the building's structure. When water vapour condenses, the water runs down windows and walls, and causes mould, health problems, and even damage to the structure of the home.

People themselves are a major source of the moisture in the air inside a building. Breath is moist and sweat evaporates; one person gives off 250ml (½ pint) of water during eight hours of sleep, and three times as much during an active day.

Domestic activities create even more moisture. Cooking, washing up, bathing, washing and drying clothes can create as much as a further 10 to 12 litres (about 3 gallons) of water a day, and every litre of fuel burnt in a flueless oil or paraffin (kerosene) heater gives off roughly another litre of water vapour.

The air in the house is expected to soak up all this extra moisture invisibly. It may not be able to manage unaided. However, a combination of improved insulation and controlled ventilation will help eliminate condensation. An electric dehumidifier can also help in soaking up excess moisture.

ABOVE: A significant cause of condensation in the kitchen is cooking. Steam rises from pans and the vapour then condenses, forming droplets on walls and ceilings.

ABOVE: Constant condensation ruins paintwork and will eventually cause wooden window frames and sills to rot, unless action is taken to increase ventilation.

PROVIDING GOOD INSULATION

Good insulation reduces the rate at which expensive domestic heat escapes through the fabric of your home and helps to protect vulnerable plumbing systems from damage during cold weather. The different parts of your home can be insulated by various methods, and most jobs can be handled by a competent person.

ROOFS AND PIPEWORK

The roof is a good place to start your insulation project. This is where pipework is at greatest risk of freezing, so pipes must be tackled as well. The main options for roof insulation are loose-fill, blanket and slab insulation, and pipes are best insulated with foam taped around them.

WALLS

The best solution for cavity walls is a job that must be left to the professionals. Despite the extra outlay, the work is very cost-effective, and you can expect to see a return on your investment after a few years. The usual procedure is to pump foam, pellets or mineral fibres into the cavity through holes drilled in the outer leaf of the wall. Make sure that the work is carried out by an approved contractor.

Applying insulation to the inner faces of walls is well within the scope of most people. One possibility is to use thermal plasterboard (gypsum board) to dry-line external walls. Another is to add a framework of wood strips to the wall, infill with slab or blanket insulation and face it with plasterboard. To prevent condensation, plastic sheeting should be stapled to the insulating material.

FLOORS, DOORS AND WINDOWS

Suspended floors can be insulated by fixing sheets of rigid polystyrene (plastic foam) between the joists, and solid floors can be lined with a vapour

ABOVE: Installing cavity wall insulation is a specialist job that can take up to three days.

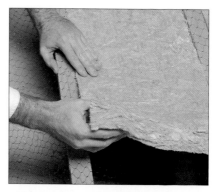

ABOVE: You can insulate a suspended floor by laying loft (attic) or wall insulation batts between the joists.

ABOVE: Glass is an extremely poor insulator, and double glazing can cut down on heat loss. It can also help to reduce noise penetration from outside and will give added security against burglars.

ABOVE: To control ventilation in steamy rooms, such as kitchens and bathrooms, extractor fans can be fitted. The types linked to humidity detectors are ideal, as they activate automatically.

barrier of heavy-duty plastic sheeting, topped with a floating floor of tongued-and-grooved chipboard (particle board) panels. Draughty floorboards can easily be repaired by applying silicone sealant (caulking) to small cracks, or by tapping slivers of wood into larger gaps.

Doors and windows are the two main sources of draughts in the home, and many products have been designed to deal with the problem. For example, gaps under doors and around windows can be sealed with draught excluder strips. Some are self-adhesive and easy to apply, while others can be fixed with screws. Make sure you choose the correct size for your doors and windows.

Windows can also be insulated by installing double glazing, either as a thin film stuck to each window frame or by fitting sliding units on to separate tracks within the window frames.

PROVIDING GOOD VENTILATION

A free flow of fresh air, ventilation is essential in a home, not only for humans to breathe, but also to prevent condensation occurring. There are many types of extractor fan that will help air to circulate. These can be fitted to ceilings, windows and walls, and can be installed by any competent do-it-yourselfer. For underfloor ventilation, airbricks are a good solution: ideally there should be an airbrick every 2m (6ft) along an external wall.

OVERCOMING DAMP

The best way of dealing with damp is to install a damp-proof course, but seek professional guidance before carrying out this work yourself. Other solutions include waterproofing exterior walls, installing ventilation fans and buying an electric dehumidifier.

MATERIALS &
EQUIPMENT

There are three basic aspects involved in saving energy in your home: insulation to prevent heat from escaping; draughtproofing to prevent cold air from seeping into your home; and ventilation to prevent condensation from forming and causing problems. Various types of insulation material are made to cope with different situations; all are easy to use. Likewise, draughtproofing materials are easy to install, although ventilation devices require a bit more effort to fit. None of this work is beyond any competent do-it-yourselfer equipped with a relatively small collection of basic tools. As with all do-it-yourself work, due regard for your own safety, and that of others who may be nearby, is essential.

INSULATION MATERIALS

Before thinking about individual types of insulation, it is important to understand the concept of cost-effectiveness. Insulation costs money to install, and can bring benefits in two main ways.

It can reduce heating bills, since the home will waste less heat and the same internal temperatures can be maintained without burning so much fuel. The annual saving on the heating bill will therefore "pay back" the cost of the extra insulation. Also, when replacing a heating system, having better standards of insulation allows

a less powerful, and less expensive, boiler to be used – an indirect saving, but valuable none the less.

ESSENTIAL BUYS

Good insulation need not mean great expenditure. The most effective items are relatively cheap and could save you a great deal in the long term. Any water storage tanks in the roof must be insulated to protect them from freezing. Padded jackets are available for the purpose. Likewise, any exposed pipework in the roof should be fitted with insulating sleeves.

ABOVE: Fix reflective foil between rafters to act as a vapour barrier over insulation.

ABOVE: Split foam pipe insulation comes in sizes to match standard pipe diameters.

ABOVE: Secure an insulation blanket to a hot water cylinder.

ABOVE: Insulate a cold water cistern with a purpose-made jacket.

LAYING LOOSE-FILL INSULATION

Lay loose-fill insulation by pouring the material between the joists. Spread it out so that it is level with the tops of the joists to ensure a thick and effective layer.

LOOSE-FILL INSULATION

This is sold by the bag and is simply poured between the joists and levelled off with their top surfaces. The dustier varieties, such as vermiculite, can be unpleasant to work with.

BLANKET INSULATION

This consists of rolls of glass fibre, mineral fibre or rock fibre, in standard widths to unroll between the joists. A typical roll length would be 6–8m (20–26ft), but short lengths are also available, known as batts. Always wear a face mask, gloves and protective clothing when laying the insulation.

SLAB INSULATION

These products are light and easy to handle, but as with the blanket versions some types may cause skin irritation. The slab widths match common joist spacings.

LAYING BLANKET INSULATION

If the roof of the house is pitched (sloping), blanket insulation can be laid over the loft (attic) floor. This is one of the most cost-effective forms of insulation.

PAY-BACK PERIODS

Hot water cylinder jacket *****
   Pay-back period: less than 1 year.
Loft (attic) insulation ****
   Pay-back period: 1–2 years.
Reflective radiator foil ****
   Pay-back period: 1–2 years.
Draught excluders ***
   Pay-back period: 2–3 years.
Flat roof insulation **(*)
   Pay-back period: 2–4 years.
Floor insulation **
   Pay-back period: 3–5 years.
Cavity wall insulation **
   Pay-back period: around 5 years.
Double glazing **(*)
   Pay-back period: 5 years or more.
Solid wall insulation *
   Pay-back period: over 10 years.

* Star rating indicates cost-effectiveness.

DRAUGHT EXCLUDERS

Draught excluder strips are an inexpensive method of sealing gaps around windows and doors. The strips are self-adhesive and easy to apply, although foam strips offer variable levels of success. Avoid the cheapest varieties, as they may soon become compressed and will not do the job properly. Look for products that are guaranteed for between two and five years. These will be easy to remove and replace if you wish to upgrade the draughtproofing system.

Rubber strips, commonly with E- or P-shaped profiles, are dearer, but are better in terms of performance and longevity. Normally, casement windows are easier to draughtproof than the sash variety.

The most effective way of keeping draughts out at the sides of sashes is to fix nylon pile brush strips to the window frame. The top and bottom do not need special treatment, as any of the products recommended for casement windows can be used.

The gap between the bottom of a door and the threshold (saddle) can be draughtproofed by attaching a solid blade or brush strip to the bottom edge of the door, so that it meets the floor or sill, or by fixing a special strip across the threshold so that it is in contact with the underside of the door.

Unused chimneys can be sealed, or a temporary solution is to block off the flue with a "balloon" device which can be removed when a fire is needed.

ABOVE: A metal draughtproofing strip can be fixed to a door frame, such as the example shown here, a V-strip type. The insert shows where the brush strip should be fixed.

ABOVE: A brush-type strip fitted at the base of the door works well on uneven surfaces.

ABOVE: A flexible rubber blade held in a plastic or aluminium extrusion, secured by screws.

EXTRACTOR FANS AND AIRBRICKS

There are several options for ensuring a constant circulation of air in the home. Each works by providing ventilation, thus preventing condensation and its associated problems.

Extractor fans can be fitted in ceilings, windows or walls. Ceiling fans are particularly effective in bathrooms and kitchens, where warm water vapour rises. Window fans need care when installing; you can either cut a hole in a single-glazed window or order a new pane with the hole already cut by a glass supplier. Wall extractor fans are fixed to an outside wall. Always check for pipes before cutting into brickwork.

Airbricks are installed into external walls to ventilate the space below suspended wooden floors.

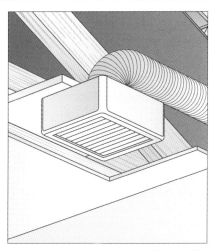

ABOVE: A ceiling-mounted extractor fan works by extracting the moist air that tends to collect just below the ceiling. A fan like this extracts this air to an outlet.

ABOVE: It is best to install a wall extractor fan as high as possible, where rising steam collects. Employ an electrician if you are unsure about how to install the wiring.

ABOVE: An airbrick contains perforated openings that allow ventilation in rooms and under wooden floors. It is important to keep them clear of earth, leaves and other debris, so clean them regularly.

TOOLS

Measuring and marking out are common tasks. A retractable steel measuring tape will take care of the former, while a combination square will allow you to mark cutting lines at 90 and 45 degrees. A craft knife can be used for marking the cutting lines as well as for cutting soft sheet materials.

A spirit (carpenter's) level is essential for finding a true horizontal or vertical.

For driving nails, a claw hammer is the ideal general-purpose tool, but for small pins (brads), the narrow end of a cross-pein hammer is better. You will need a nail punch to punch nail heads below the surface of the work, and a nail puller to remove nails or pins.

Various sizes of screwdriver for slotted, Phillips and Pozidriv screws will be necessary, while an adjustable spanner can be used on nuts and bolts.

Saws are also essential. Choose a general-purpose hand saw for large sections of wood and a tenon saw for smaller work. A mitre box will allow you to make 45-degree cuts.

For drilling holes, a cordless drill will be most convenient.

Use a jack plane for shaping wood, and bevel-edged chisels to make cutouts and recesses. Abrasive paper is essential for giving a final finish to wood.

When filling cracks and holes, use a putty knife for small repairs and a small trowel for larger ones. Use a caulking gun to apply silicone sealants.

A heavy-duty stapler is ideal for securing netting to joists for insulating.

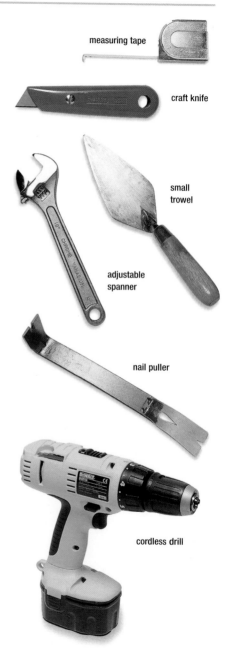

measuring tape

craft knife

small trowel

adjustable spanner

nail puller

cordless drill

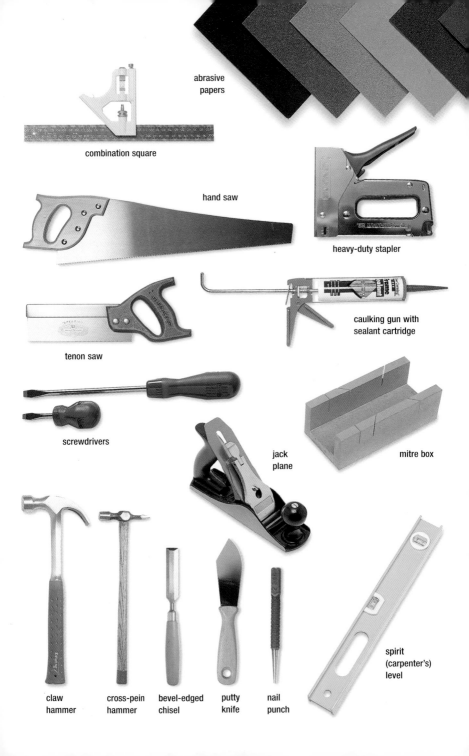

abrasive papers

combination square

hand saw

heavy-duty stapler

tenon saw

caulking gun with sealant cartridge

screwdrivers

jack plane

mitre box

claw hammer

cross-pein hammer

bevel-edged chisel

putty knife

nail punch

spirit (carpenter's) level

AWARENESS AND CLOTHING

A complete book could be devoted to the subject of safety in the home, and there is a wide range of equipment designed to minimize our capacity for hurting ourselves. Nevertheless, there is one requirement that we cannot buy, without which all that equipment is virtually useless, namely concentration. This is particularly important when working alone.

AWARENESS

Concentration is essential when using any form of power tool, especially a saw, where one slip can mean the loss of a finger, or worse. The dangers of accidents involving electricity are well documented, as are those involving falls from ladders, spillages of toxic materials, and burns and injuries caused by contact with fire or abrasive surfaces. In almost every case, there is a loss of concentration, coupled with poor work practices and inadequate protective clothing or equipment. So, although the items shown here are all useful forms of protection, concentrating on what you are doing is the best advice to prevent accidents from occurring around the home.

CLOTHING

Overalls are a good investment because they not only protect clothing, but also most are designed to be close-fitting to prevent accidental contact with moving machinery. Industrial gloves, although not worn by those engaged in fine work, can provide very useful protection against cuts and bruises when doing rougher jobs. Similarly, safety boots should be worn when heavy lifting or the use of machinery is involved.

Knee pads are necessary for comfort when working on a floor or carrying out any other job that requires a lot of kneeling. They will also protect the wearer from injury if a nail or similar projection is knelt on accidentally.

Finally, a bump cap is worth considering. This will protect the head from minor injuries and bumps, but is not so cumbersome as the hard hat required on building sites. It is ideal for working in the close confines of a roof.

ABOVE: Wear overalls to protect your clothes when carrying out any dirty or dusty job. Disposable types are available for one-off jobs.

ABOVE: A pair of thick gloves will be essential when handling rough materials such as sawn wood or sharp objects such as broken glass. Make sure they fit well.

ABOVE: If you have to do a job that involves a lot of kneeling, rubber knee pads will be invaluable. They provide comfort and protection from sharp projections such as nail heads.

ABOVE: Safety boots with steel caps will protect your feet from injury when working with heavy items such as large sections of wood, bricks and concrete blocks.

ABOVE: When working in situations where you may hit your head accidentally, the bump cap will provide protection without being as cumbersome as a conventional hard hat.

SAFETY

Make sure you have the appropriate safety equipment to hand when carrying out do-it-yourself tasks, and always use it. Doing so can prevent nasty accidents and serious injury.

FIRST AID

Keeping a basic first aid kit is a common and wise precaution even before any do-it-yourself work is envisaged. It should always be kept where it can be reached easily.

You can buy a home first aid kit that will contain all the necessary items to cope with minor injuries, or you can assemble your own, keeping it in a plastic box with an airtight lid.

You should include items such as bandages, plasters, wound dressings, antiseptic cream, eye pads, scissors, tweezers and pins.

If you have cause to use your first aid kit, replace the items you have removed as soon as possible.

AIRBORNE DANGERS

When you are working with wood, the most common airborne danger is dust, mainly from sawing and sanding. This can do long-term damage to the lungs.

A simple face mask, however, will offer adequate protection for occasional jobs. These can also be purchased for protection against fumes, such as from solvents, which can be very harmful. Dust, of course, also affects the eyes, so it is worth investing in a pair of impact-resistant goggles, which will protect the wearer from both fine dust and flying debris. Full facial protection is available as a powered respirator for those working in dusty conditions over long periods.

When carrying out insulation work it is particularly important to wear a face mask to avoid inhaling glass fibre, mineral wool or loose-fill material. It is also important to wear gloves to avoid skin irritation.

RIGHT: Typical personal safety equipment – first aid kit, impact-resistant safety spectacles, ear protectors, two types of dust mask and sturdy industrial-type gloves.

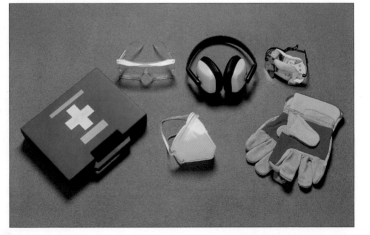

LEFT: A simple circuit breaker can save a life by cutting off the power to faulty equipment.

ELECTRICAL SAFETY

If used incorrectly, electrical equipment can be life-threatening, and the dangers of fire are obvious. Always treat the former with respect, and take sensible precautions against the latter.

Some tools have removable switches that allow the user to immobilize them and prevent any unauthorized use.

To safeguard against electrocution, which can occur if the flex (power cord) is faulty or is cut accidentally, the ideal precaution is a residual current device (RCD). This is simply plugged into the main supply socket (electrical outlet) before the flex and will give complete protection to the user.

The danger of electrocution or damage caused by accidentally drilling into an existing cable or pipe can be largely prevented by using an electronic pipe and cable detector, which will locate and differentiate between metal pipes, wooden studs and live wires through plaster and concrete to a depth of approximately 50mm (2in). These are not too expensive and will be very useful around the home.

SAFE ACCESS

Steps and ladders can be hazardous, so make sure they are in good condition. Accessories include a ladder stay, which spreads the weight of the ladder

ABOVE: A ladder platform will provide a firm footing, especially if heavy footwear is worn.

ABOVE: Platforms supported by trestles, or step-ladders, are the safest way to work at a height.

across a vertical surface, such as a wall, to prevent slippage; and a standing platform, which is used to provide a more comfortable and safer surface to stand on. The last often has a ribbed rubber surface and can be attached to the rungs of almost all ladders. Even more stable is a movable workstation or a board or staging slung between two pairs of steps or trestles. These can often be used with a safety rail, which prevents the operator from falling even if a slip occurs.

INSULATION & DRAUGHTPROOFING

Heat rises, so the most important area of your home to insulate is the roof. Fortunately, this is very easy to do, although working in a small roof space can be difficult. Keeping the heat below the ceiling may have unforeseen consequences, however, in that any pipes and water tanks in the roof may freeze, so these too must be wrapped in insulating material. Once you have dealt with the roof, turn your attention to the walls and floors, since both can be insulated to provide a real bonus in energy saving. Floors not only act as heat sinks, but if boarded, they can allow in cold draughts. Sealing the gaps between boards will make your rooms feel cosy, as will draughtproofing the doors and windows. For extra comfort, opt for double glazing.

INSULATING ROOFS

In a building with a pitched (sloping) roof, where the loft (attic) space is used only for storage, it is usual to insulate the loft floor. To do this, use either blankets of glass fibre or mineral wool, sold by the roll, or else use loose-fill material (vermiculite, a lightweight expanded mineral, is the most widely used). Some kinds of loose-fill insulation, usually mineral wool or fireproofed cellulose fibres, can be blown into the loft by specialist professional contractors.

Blanket materials are generally easier to handle than loose-fill types unless the loft is awkwardly shaped, contains a lot of obstructions or has irregular joist spacings. The rolls are generally 600mm (24in) wide to match standard joist spacing, and common thicknesses are 100mm (4in) and 150mm (6in).

Choose the latter unless there is already thin sonic loft insulation, and ensure that it is laid with eaves baffles to allow adequate ventilation of the loft, otherwise condensation may form and lead to rotting of the wood. It is essential to wear protective clothing when handling glass fibre insulation. Wear a face mask, gloves and cover any exposed skin with suitable clothing.

Apart from being awkward to handle, loose-fill materials have another drawback. To be as effective as blanket types, they need laying to a greater depth – usually at least an extra 25mm (1in). With few ceiling joists being deeper than about 150mm (6in), there is nothing to contain the insulation and allow for maintenance access, unless strips of wood are fixed along the top edge of every joist.

LAYING LOOSE-FILL INSULATION

1 Lay loose-fill insulation by pouring the material between the joists. Prevent it from running out at the eaves by fixing lengths of wood between the joists.

2 Level it off with a spreader, which you can make from chipboard (particle board). You may need to add strips of wood to the joists to obtain the required depth of insulation.

LAYING BLANKET ROOF INSULATION

1 Clear all stored items from the loft (attic) area, then put down a sturdy kneeling board and use a heavy-duty vacuum cleaner to remove dust and debris.

2 Always put on gloves and a face mask, and wear long sleeves, to handle the insulation. Unroll it between the joists, leaving the eaves clear for ventilation.

3 Butt-join the ends of successive lengths of blanket. To cut the material to length, either use long-bladed scissors or simply tear it.

4 While working across the loft, make sure that any electrical cables are lifted clear of the insulation so they cannot overheat.

5 Insulate the upper surface of the loft hatch by wrapping a piece of blanket in plastic sheeting and stapling this to the hatch door.

6 Do not insulate under water tanks. If the tank has a lid, blanket insulation can also be wrapped around the tank and tied in place.

INSULATING PIPEWORK

When the loft (attic) floor is completely insulated, remember to insulate any water tanks and pipework within the loft, since they are now at risk of freezing. For this reason, do not lay insulation under water tanks.

FOAM PIPE INSULATION

Exposed pipework in the loft can easily be protected by covering it with proprietary foam pipe insulation. Basically, this comprises lengths of foam tubing, which have been split along the length and which come with inside diameters to match common domestic pipe sizes. All that is necessary is to open the split to allow the foam to be fitted over the pipe.

PIPE BANDAGE INSULATION

An alternative method is to use pipe bandage, but this is more labour intensive, since it must be wrapped around the pipe, although the fibrous material is useful for pipes with awkward bends. To secure it, tie each end firmly with a short length of string.

JACKETS FOR TANKS

Tanks can be insulated with proprietary jackets, or you can tie lengths of blanket insulation around them, or tape on thick rigid foam sheets. Alternatively, you can build a plywood box around the tank and fill the gap between it and the tank with loose-fill insulation material.

INSULATING PIPES WITH BANDAGE

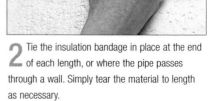

1 Pipe bandage can be used instead of foam insulation. Wrap it around the pipe in a spiral, with successive turns just overlapping. Don't leave any pipework exposed.

2 Tie the insulation bandage in place at the end of each length, or where the pipe passes through a wall. Simply tear the material to length as necessary.

INSULATING PIPES WITH FOAM

1 The quickest and easiest way of insulating pipework is to slip on lengths of foam pipe insulation, which is slit lengthways. Join the lengths with PVC (vinyl) tape.

2 To make neat joins in the insulation at corners, cut the ends at 45 degrees, using a mitre box and a carving knife or hacksaw blade. Tape the corner joint.

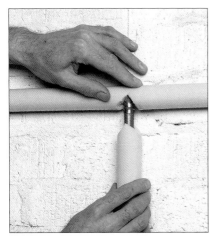

3 Make a V-shaped cutout in the insulation at a tee joint, then cut an arrow shape to match it on the end of the insulation which will cover the branch pipe.

4 As with butt and corner joints, use PVC tape to secure the sections of insulation together and prevent them from slipping out of position. In time, you may need to renew this.

BOXING-IN PIPES

Some people regard visible pipes in the home as an eyesore. Moreover, where the pipes are in rooms that are unheated, or where they run against external walls, there is a possibility that they may freeze during a severe winter. Fortunately, with a little time and minimal woodworking skills, exposed pipes can be hidden successfully from view and protected from freezing at the same time, by building boxing around them and filling it with loose-fill insulation. If the boxing is decorated to match the room, the pipes can be concealed completely. Be sure to allow for the boxwork to be easily removed in situations where it may be necessary to gain access.

ACCESSIBILITY

Bear in mind that stopcocks, drain taps, pumps, hand-operated valves and the like will need to be readily accessible and require some form of removable box system. For this reason, the boxing around them should be assembled with screws rather than nails. If a panel needs to be regularly or quickly removed, turn buttons or magnetic catches are a good idea.

BOXING BASICS

Steel anchor plates and screws can be used to secure the sides of boxing to walls, and these will be easy to remove when necessary. Battens (furring strips), either 50 x 25mm (2 x 1in) or 25 x 25mm (1 x 1in), can be used to fix boards at skirting (baseboard) level.

Disguise the boxing by decorating it to match the rest of the room. If pipework is running along a panelled or boarded wall, construct the boxing so that it follows the general theme, using similar materials and staining and varnishing the boxes accordingly.

WALL PIPES

Measure the distance the pipes project from the wall, taking account of any joints and brackets. Cut the side panels from 25mm (1in) board slightly over this measurement and to their correct length. Fix small anchor plates flush with the back edge of each panel and spaced at about 600mm (24in) intervals.

If using plywood, you may need to drill pilot holes. Hold the panels against the wall and mark the positions of the screw holes on the wall. Drill the holes and fix the panels to the wall with rawl plugs and screws.

Cut the front panel to size from 6mm ($\frac{1}{4}$in) plywood. Drill evenly spaced screw holes in the front panel and fix it in position with 19mm ($\frac{3}{4}$in) No. 6 screws. Use cup washers underneath the screw heads to protect the panel if it is likely to be removed often. Trim the edges flush with a block plane.

With horizontal pipes, arrange the boxing so that you can remove the top panel to make filling with loose-fill insulation easy. For vertical pipes, leave a small access panel at the top of the box and pour the insulation through this, tapping the boxing to make sure that it fills the void completely.

BOXING-IN WALL PIPES

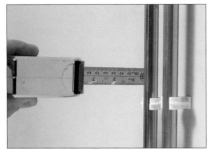

1 Measure how far the pipes protrude from the face of the wall.

2 With a pencil, mark the positions for the side batten fixings.

3 Attach the side battens, screwing them firmly into position.

4 Cut the front panel of the box to size with a jigsaw. Use 6mm (¼in) plywood.

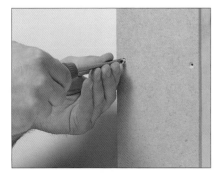

5 Drill pilot holes and screw the front panel into position, using 19mm (¾in) No. 6 screws.

6 Trim the edges of the front panel with a block plane. Add loose-fill insulation from the top.

INSULATING SOLID WALLS

House walls are the most extensive part of the whole building and absorb a lot of heat, which is why a house takes so long to warm up once it has become cold. Some of the lost heat can be retained by insulating the walls.

For solid walls, the most economical solution is to dry-line them on the inside with insulating plasterboard (gypsum board), fixed directly to the wall with panel adhesive or nailed to a supporting framework of treated wood strips. Alternatively, ordinary plasterboard sheets can be used, with insulation blanket or boards placed between the support strips and covered with a plastic vapour barrier.

INSULATING CAVITY WALLS

The cavity wall consists of two "leaves" of masonry with a gap, usually of 50mm (2in), between them. Their insulation performance can be improved by filling the cavity with insulating material. This is done by specialist installers who pump treated fibres, pellets or insulating foam into the cavity through holes drilled in the wall's outer leaf.

For wood-framed walls, the best alternative is to remove the interior finish, install insulation batts and cover these with a vapour barrier, such as plastic sheeting. Then add a new inner skin of plasterboard.

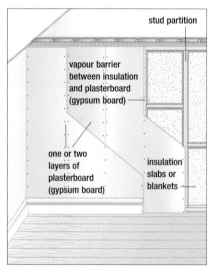

ABOVE: A wall can be insulated by erecting a stud partition wall in front of it, the void being filled with blanket or slab insulation, while two layers of plasterboard (gypsum board) are added to the framework.

stud partition

vapour barrier between insulation and plasterboard (gypsum board)

one or two layers of plasterboard (gypsum board)

insulation slabs or blankets

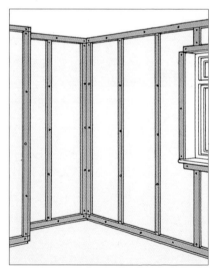

ABOVE: Fix a framework of 50 x 25mm (2 x 1in) softwood strips to the walls with masonry nails to support the edges and centres of the insulating boards.

ADDING THE DRY-LINING

1 Mark cutting lines on the board surface in pencil, then cut along the line with the insulation facing downwards, using a fine-toothed saw.

2 Use a simple lever and fulcrum to raise the boards to touch the room ceiling as they are fixed. A skirting (baseboard) will cover the gap.

3 Fix the boards by positioning them against the supporting framework so that adjacent boards meet over a strip, and nail them in place. The nail heads should just "dimple" the surface.

4 At external corners, remove a strip of the polystyrene (plastic foam) insulation as wide as the board thickness so the edges of the plasterboard (gypsum board) can meet in a butt joint.

5 Arrange the boards at external corners so that a paper-covered board edge conceals one that has its plaster core exposed. Finish off all joints with plasterboard tape and filler.

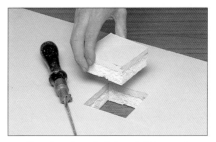

6 To make cutouts for light switch boxes, plug sockets and similar obstacles, mark their positions on the boards and cut them out with a padsaw.

INSULATING SUSPENDED FLOORS

Few people think of ground floors when considering insulation, yet a surprisingly large amount of heat can be lost through both solid and suspended wood floors. Insulating a suspended floor will involve disruptive work, since the floorboards will need lifting. However, if you are prepared to do this, the methods are very similar to laying roof insulation.

INSULATION METHODS

With suspended wood floors insulation can be fixed between the joists after lifting the floorboards. One method is to cut strips of rigid expanded polystyrene (plastic foam) and rest them on nails driven into the sides of the joists, or on battens nailed to the sides of the joists. Bear in mind that the material is very light and may be dislodged by severe draughts caused by windy weather; a few nails driven into the joists to "pinch" the edges of the insulation will help.

Another method of treating a suspended floor is to fill the gaps between joists with lengths of insulation blanket, supported on nylon garden netting stapled to the joists. Pull up the netting tightly before

LIFTING FLOORBOARDS

Unless you have a basement that allows you to reach the underside of a suspended floor, to insulate it you will have to lift all of the floorboards.

To lift a board, tap the blade of a bolster (stonecutter's) chisel into the gap between two boards, close to the end of the board you want to lift, and lever the board upward; repeat for the other side.

Continue levering until the end of the board is clear of the floor and you can insert the claw of a hammer beneath it.

Use the hammer to lever the end high enough to insert a length of wood beneath the board to hold the end clear of the floor. Continue in this way along the board until you can lift it completely.

nailing down the boards so that the blanket does not sag and let cold air through. The insulation is then covered with a vapour barrier.

USING INSULATION BLANKET

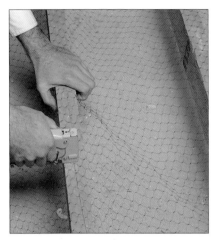

1 To insulate the void beneath a wooden floor, lift all the floorboards. Then drape lengths of garden netting loosely over the joists and staple them in place.

2 Lay lengths of loft (attic) insulation blanket or wall insulation batts in the "hammocks" between the joists. If the netting sags, pull it up a little and staple it again.

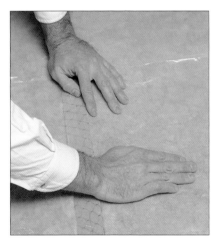

3 To prevent moisture from the house condensing within the insulation, cover the insulation with a vapour barrier of heavy-duty plastic sheeting.

4 Re-lay the floorboards by nailing them to the joists. Take this opportunity to close up any joints between the boards for a neat finish and to cut down draughts.

INSULATING SOLID FLOORS

With direct-to-ground concrete floors (slab on grade), the commonest method of insulation involves lining the floor with a vapour barrier of heavy-duty plastic sheeting, and installing a floating floor of tongued-and-grooved chipboard (particle board) panels. If additional insulation is required, place rigid polystyrene (plastic foam) insulation boards directly on top of the vapour barrier, then lay the new flooring on top of them.

Treat damp floors with one or two coats of a proprietary damp-proofing liquid and allow to dry before laying the vapour barrier. A gap of 9mm (⅜in) should be left between the chipboard and the wall to allow for expansion. This gap will not be noticeable once a new skirting (baseboard) is installed. The layer of trapped air under the floating floor will help keep the area warm.

Since the new floor will be at a raised level, any doors will need to be removed and planed down to a smaller size. Also, the flooring will either have to be cut to fit around architraves (door trim), or the architraves will have to be shortened so that the flooring fits beneath them.

LAYING A FLOATING FLOOR

1 Remove the skirtings (baseboards) and put down heavy-duty plastic sheets. Tape the sheets to the walls; they will be hidden behind the skirting later. Then butt-joint 25mm (1in) polystyrene (plastic foam) insulation boards over the floor, staggering the joints in adjacent rows.

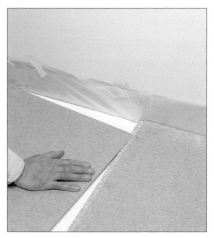

2 Cover the polystyrene insulation board with tongued-and-grooved flooring-grade boards. Use cut pieces as necessary at the ends of rows, and add a tapered threshold (saddle) strip at the door. When finished, replace the skirtings with hammer and nails.

DRAUGHTPROOFING FLOORS

Gaps between the boards of a suspended wooden floor can allow cold draughts to enter a room. There are various methods for coping with this problem, depending on the size of the gaps and whether you want the boards exposed as a decorative feature, or are happy to conceal them beneath a floorcovering.

EXPOSED FLOORBOARDS

Large gaps in floorboards can be filled with strips of wood, carefully cut to fit tightly. Spread adhesive on the sides of each strip and tap it into the gap. Allow the glue to set, then plane down the strip so that it is flush with the surrounding floor. The strips can then be stained to match the colour of the other floorboards.

In severe cases, and if you want the boards to be exposed, you may have no option but to lift all of the boards and re-lay them, butting them tightly together as you do so. You can hire special flooring clamps for this purpose, which attach to the joists and allow you to push the boards tightly together before you nail them down. ▶

TIP

A papier-mâché mix made from pieces of newspaper and a thick solution of wallpaper paste can be used to repair small holes in floorboards. Add woodstain to match the surrounding boards, then sand the repair smooth when dry.

ABOVE: Tap slivers of wood in place to cure draughts through large gaps. Leave the repair slightly proud of the surface. Once the glue has set, sand down the raised area to a smooth finish with a power sander or planer.

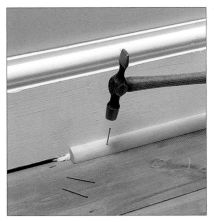

ABOVE: Stop draughts at skirting (baseboard) level by filling any gaps with silicone sealant (caulking) and covering with quadrant (quarter-round) moulding. Secure the quadrant moulding with pins.

COVERED FLOORS

Where there are large gaps between floorboards, and especially if the boards themselves are in poor condition, you can cover the floor with sheets of hardboard to provide a sound surface for carpeting or some other form of floorcovering. At the same time, this sub-floor will eliminate draughts.

Before laying, condition the hardboard by spraying the textured side of each sheet with 450ml (¾ pint) of water. Stack the sheets back-to-back and flat, separated by strips of wood, on the floor of the room where they are to be laid. Leave them for 48 hours, until they are completely dry.

Begin laying the hardboard sheets in the corner of the room farthest from the door, fixing each sheet in place with 19mm (¾in) annular (spiral) flooring nails. Start to nail 12mm (½in) from the skirting (baseboard) edge. To ensure the boards lie flat, work across the surface in a pyramid sequence, spacing the nails 150mm (6in) apart along the edges and 230mm (9in) apart in the middle.

Butt boards edge to edge to complete the first row, nailing the meeting edges first. Use the offcut (scrap) from the first row to start the next row, and continue in this way, staggering the joins between rows.

If boards are in really poor condition, you may be better off replacing them completely with tongued-and-grooved chipboard (particle board) panels, which will eliminate draughts.

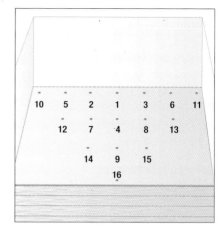

ABOVE: Nail across a hardboard sheet in a pyramid sequence to avoid creating bulges. Nails should be 150mm (6in) apart along the edges and 230mm (9in) apart in the middle.

LAYING A HARDBOARD SUB-FLOOR

1 Condition the hardboard sheets by brushing or spraying them with water, and leave them for 48 hours before laying.

CARPET

If the gaps between boards are narrow, and you don't want the boards to be exposed, the easiest method of coping with a draughty floor is to lay fitted carpet with a good underlay.

Put down the underlay and cover with double-sided adhesive tape. Unroll the carpet and butt the edges up against the walls of the room and ensure that the carpet is lying flat. Trim the edges against the skirtings (baseboards) and tape them down.

Laying carpet will effectively block the passage of air through the floor. For added protection, you can repair any major gaps between the boards with a silicone sealant (caulking).

LAYING CARPET

When the gaps between floorboards are relatively narrow, simply laying a good-quality, thick underlay beneath the carpet will prevent draughts from being a problem.

2 To ensure a secure fixing, use annular (spiral) flooring nails. A piece of wood cut to size will allow you to space nails correctly and rapidly.

3 Use the offcut (scrap) from each row to start the next so that joins are staggered.

DRAUGHTPROOFING DOORS

Ill-fitting doors are a major source of heat loss, as well as causing cold draughts. Fitting efficient draught stripping around them will reduce the losses and cut down the draughts, and is a simple job to carry out.

Doors are best draughtproofed with pin-on (tack-on) plastic or sprung metal strips or types containing a compressible rubber seal. Special draught excluders are available for door thresholds (saddles), and can be fitted to the door bottom or across the threshold. There are even excluders designed to fit over letter plate openings.

REMEMBER VENTILATION

Don't forget that draughtproofing a home will close off many "unofficial" sources of ventilation, turning it into a well-sealed box. Fuel-burning appliances such as boilers and room heaters must have an adequate source of fresh air to burn safely, so it is wise to ask a fuel supplier to check that there is adequate ventilation in rooms containing such appliances. Often a ventilator in a window pane will solve the problem. However, you may need to take more drastic steps, such as fitting an airbrick into a wall with a vent cover that can be opened and closed.

Efficient draughtproofing may also increase condensation, especially in kitchens and bathrooms. This can be prevented by providing controlled ventilation in these rooms with an extractor fan.

ABOVE: Letter plate openings can be draught-proofed in a variety of ways. You can fit a hinged plate to the inside to provide extra protection. Alternatively, rubber and brush seals are available that will also do the job.

ABOVE: Draughts may not only pass around doors, but also through them. The problem is quite easy to solve. Keyhole covers are inexpensive. Many locks intended for external doors are provided with them as standard.

1 The simplest type of door-bottom draught excluder is a brush seal mounted in a wood or plastic strip. Simply cut it to length and screw it on to the foot of the door.

2 Alternatively, fit a threshold (saddle) strip. Cut the metal bar to length and screw it to the sill, then fit the compressible rubber sealing strip in the channel.

3 Draughtproof a letter plate opening by screwing on a special brush seal. Check beforehand that it does not foul the letter plate flap if this opens inwards.

4 Draughtproof the sides and top of the door frame by pinning (tacking) on lengths of plastic or sprung metal sealing strip. Pin the edge farthest from the door stop bead.

5 Alternatively, stick lengths of self-adhesive foam excluder to the stop bead against which the door closes. At the hinge side, stick the foam to the frame.

6 A third option is to use lengths of self-adhesive brush strip excluder. These three types can also be used for draughtproofing hinged casement windows.

DRAUGHTPROOFING WINDOWS

Windows are a major source of draughts in the home and are responsible for about ten per cent of heat loss. Many products have been designed to deal with these problems, but they vary in cost-effectiveness. The simplest are draught excluder strips, similar to those used for doors, while the most expensive remedy is to replace single-glazed units with double glazing. The latter will provide a considerable degree of comfort, as well as reducing sound transmission, but it may take up to 20 years to recoup your investment in terms of energy savings.

SEALING THE GAPS

You can choose from a variety of draught stripping products for windows, but some are more effective on certain types of window than others. For example, modern self-adhesive foams are much more efficient and longer lasting than older types, and are ideal for hinged casement windows. Simply stick strips around the rebate (rabbet) of the frame so that the opening casement compresses them when closed.

Sash windows, however, are not so easy to treat. The best solution is to use the same type of plastic or sprung metal strips that are suitable for doors. These can be pinned (tacked) around the frame to provide a seal against the sliding sashes. The job can be completed by attaching strips of self-adhesive foam to the top edge of the upper sash and bottom edge of the lower sash, so that these seal against the frame.

SASH WINDOWS

1 To fit a sprung metal strip excluder to a sliding sash window, first prise off the staff bead (window stop) that holds the inner sash in position, and swing it out.

4 Use the special wheeled springing tool provided with the draught excluder to make a small groove in the strip, causing it to spring outwards to press against the sash.

2 Measure the length of strip needed to fit the height of the window, and cut it to length with a pair of scissors. Beware of the sharp edges of the metal.

3 Pin (tack) the strip to the side of the frame so it will press against the edge of the sliding sash. Drive the pin through the edge facing towards the room.

5 Pin a length of the strip along the inner face of the top sash meeting rail (mullion), and "spring" it so it presses against the outer face of the bottom sash rail.

6 You can draughtproof the bottom edge of the lower sash and the top edge of the upper one by sticking on lengths of self-adhesive foam draught excluder.

DOUBLE GLAZING

The glass in windows is the least efficient part of the house at keeping heat in, and the only way of cutting this heat loss while still being able to see out is to add another layer of glass. Double glazing can be done in two ways: existing single panes of glass can be replaced with special double-glazed panes called sealed units, or a second pane can be installed inside the existing one – so-called secondary glazing.

SECONDARY GLAZING

This is the only practical form of double glazing for the do-it-yourselfer, and it is relatively inexpensive. There are dozens of types available, providing hinged and sliding inner panes that blend in well with most types of window; similar systems are also available from professional installers. The panes are either fixed directly to the window frame, or fitted within the window reveal on special tracks.

SLIDING UNITS

Do-it-yourself secondary glazing systems come in kit form and are easy to install. The kits provide enough materials to cover a range of window sizes; all you need do is cut the lengths of special track to fit within the window reveal and screw them in place. You do have to provide your own glass, however, and careful measurements must be taken so that you can order this from your local glass supplier. Then all you need do is fit the glazing gaskets and insert the panes in the tracks.

FITTING SLIDING UNITS

1 Measure the height and width of the window reveal at each side. If the figures differ, work from the smaller measurements for height and width. Cut the track sections to size.

4 When positioning the bottom track on the windowsill, use a straightedge and a spirit (carpenter's) level to check that it is perfectly aligned with the top track.

2 Offer up the side track sections and screw them to the window reveal. Use thin packing pieces to get them truly vertical if the walls are out of square.

3 Next, secure the top track section in place. Screw it directly to a wooden lintel or pre-drill holes in a concrete beam and insert plastic wall plugs first.

5 Measure up for the glass as directed in the kit manufacturer's instructions, and order the glass. Fit cut lengths of glazing gasket to the edges of each pane.

6 Fit the first pane into the track by inserting its top edge in the top channel, and then lowering its bottom edge. Repeat the procedure for the other pane.

CLEAR FILM

There is a particularly cheap form
of secondary glazing that involves
attaching a clear PVC (vinyl) film to the
inside of the window with double-sided
adhesive tape. This can be discarded
during the summer months and fresh
film applied for the winter.

A sturdier option is acrylic sheet.
If you opt for this method, make sure
that at least one window is easy to
open in case of an emergency.

DON'T FORGET THE DOORS

Heat is lost through external doors too,
and solid doors are best. If you prefer a
glazed door, however, opt for a modern
replacement fitted with a sealed double-
glazing unit. You can reduce heat loss
still further with an enclosed porch.

FITTING THIN-FILM SECONDARY GLAZING

1 Start by sticking lengths of double-sided
adhesive tape to the window frame, about
12mm (½in) in from the surrounding masonry.

2 Press the film on to the tape, pulling it as taut
as possible. Then play hot air from a hairdrier
over it to tighten it up and pull out any wrinkles.

3 When the film is even and wrinkle-free, trim
off the excess all the way around the window
with a sharp knife.

APPLYING SEALANTS

Silicone sealants (caulking) are good for filling large or irregularly shaped gaps around windows and doors. They come in white, brown and clear versions. Use a caulking gun for ease of application, although products that do not require a gun are also available.

To make a repair with silicone sealant, clean the frame rebate (rabbet) and apply the sealant to the fixed frame. Brush soapy water on to the closing edge of the window or door. Close and immediately open the door. The soapy water acts as a release agent, preventing the door or window from sticking to the sealant.

Because silicone sealants are flexible, they will absorb movement in the structure of your home that otherwise would produce cracking. For particularly large gaps around frames, you can use an expanding foam filler.

ABOVE: Fill cracks between the window frame and plasterwork with silicone sealant (caulking).

ABOVE: You can also use silicone sealant outdoors to seal gaps between frames and masonry where a rigid filler might crack.

ABOVE: Coloured silicone sealants can be used to blend in with their surroundings – or you can paint over them when a skin has formed.

VENTILATION

You can go too far in draughtproofing your home; if you seal up all the sources of outside air, you will prevent moist air from being carried away. This will cause condensation to form on any cold surfaces, such as windows, tiles and exterior walls. In severe cases, this can result in mould growth and even damage to the structure of your home. Moreover, a lack of airflow can cause problems with certain types of heater. The ideal is to keep out the cold draughts, but provide a sufficient flow of air to prevent condensation and ensure the efficient operation of heaters. The judicious use of manual vents, airbricks and electric extractor fans will provide all the ventilation you need without making you feel chilly.

FITTING A CEILING EXTRACTOR FAN

An extractor fan provides positive ventilation where it is needed, in a kitchen or bathroom, removing stale or moist air before it can cause a problem. There are three places you can fit an extractor fan: in a window, in a wall or in the ceiling, where ducts carry the stale air to the outside. In a kitchen, an extracting cooker hood can serve the same function, provided it is ducted to the outside; a recirculating cooker hood only filters the air.

It is important that an extractor fan is positioned so that the replacement air, which normally will come through and around the door leading to the remainder of the house, is drawn through the room and across the problem area. In a kitchen, the problem areas are the cooker and the sink; in a bathroom, they are the lavatory and shower unit.

Ceiling-mounted extractor fans are particularly efficient in bathrooms and kitchens, since the warm moist air will tend to collect just below the ceiling. Moreover, fitting the fan in the ceiling often makes for an easier installation, since all you need do is cut a circular hole in the ceiling with a padsaw, taking care to avoid the ceiling joists. From the fan, plastic ducting needs to be taken to an outside wall or to the eaves, where it is connected to an outlet. On no account allow it to discharge into the roof.

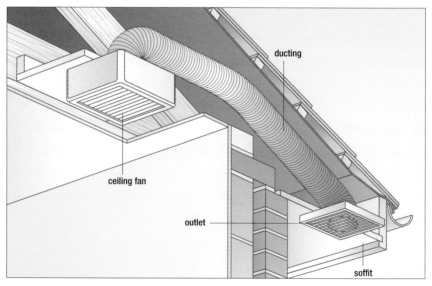

ducting

ceiling fan

outlet

soffit

ABOVE: Fit an extractor fan in the ceiling so that it discharges via a duct to a hole with an outlet at the soffit.

FITTING A WINDOW EXTRACTOR FAN

If a simple window ventilator already exists in a fixed window, you may be able to replace it with an extractor fan. If not, you will have to cut a hole in one of the window panes. However, this will not be possible if the glass is toughened or laminated. The same applies to double-glazed units; they must be ordered with the hole pre-cut.

The only window you can cut a hole in is one made from normal glass in a single-glazed frame, and even here you may prefer to order a new pane from a glass supplier with the hole already cut. That way, the only work you will have to do is to take out the old pane and fit the new one.

Fit the extractor fan near the top of the window, since warm, moist air rises and it will do the most good at high level. Also, this will keep the fan away from inquisitive children, who may be tempted to push things into it.

To cut the hole in the glass yourself, you will need a beam circle cutter as well as a normal glass cutter. Use the beam cutter to score two circles: one the correct size for the extractor fan, and one slightly smaller inside it. Then use the normal glass cutter to make cross-hatched lines inside the inner circle, and single radial lines between the two circles. Tap out the glass from the inner circle, then use the glass breaker rack on the glass cutter to snap off the remaining margin of glass. Smooth the edge with fine abrasive paper wrapped around a circular tool handle or piece of thick dowelling rod. Once you have a hole of the correct size, fitting a window fan is simply a matter of following the instructions.

ABOVE: If the window was fitted originally with a simple ventilator unit such as this one, you may be able to remove it and fit an extractor fan in the existing hole.

ABOVE: If no ventilator is fitted, you will need to cut a hole in the glass to fit an extractor fan. For this, you will need a special tool known as a beam circle cutter.

FITTING A WALL EXTRACTOR FAN

Most designs of extractor fan will require a circular hole to be cut through the house wall. The best tool to use for this is a heavy-duty electric drill fitted with a core drill bit, both of which you can hire. These will cut a hole of exactly the right size. Make holes in both leaves of a cavity wall and fit the sleeve supplied with the extractor fan. Some fans require a rectangular hole to be cut, which may mean removing one or more whole bricks. Take care when doing this; cut through the mortar joints around the bricks with a cold chisel and club (spalling) hammer, and try to ease the bricks out in one piece. Keep as much debris as possible out of the wall cavity, since this could bridge the cavity and lead to damp problems. Once the sleeve for the fan is in place, make good the brickwork and plaster.

Fitting the fan is easy – simply drill holes for wall plugs to take the fan on the inside wall, and fit the outlet on the outer wall.

WIRING

An extractor fan needs to be wired up via a fused connection unit to the nearest power supply circuit. If you are not sure how to do this, employ a qualified electrician to do the job. In a bathroom or shower room, with no opening window, a fan is a compulsory requirement and it must be wired via the light switch so that it comes on with the light and remains on for 15 minutes afterwards.

1 The first step when fitting a wall-mounted extractor fan is to mark the exact position of the wall sleeve. Place the fan near the top of the wall for the best performance.

4 Offer up the extractor and mark its fixing-hole positions on the wall. Drill these and fit them with wall plugs so that you can screw the extractor to the wall surface.

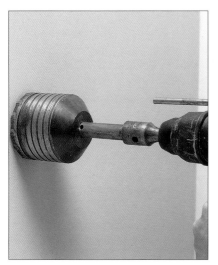

2 Use a core drill bit, fitted to a heavy-duty electric drill, to cut a hole of the correct size through both leaves of the wall (if it is of the cavity type).

3 Check the fit of the sleeve in the hole and push it through the wall. Mark it off for length, then remove it and cut it down with a hacksaw. Replace it.

5 Wiring comes next (get help with this if necessary). Make a check that the extractor functions correctly, after which the cover of the unit can be put on.

6 Finally, fit the outlet on the outside wall. Sometimes this simply pushes into the end of the sleeve. In other cases, you may need to screw it to the wall.

FITTING EXTRA AIRBRICKS

In other rooms, fitting small "trickle" ventilators at the top of window frames and putting in extra airbricks will often supply enough ventilation to allow the moist air to disperse before condensation becomes a problem.

UNDERFLOOR VENTILATION

A suspended wooden floor consists of floorboards or sheets of flooring-grade chipboard (particle board) supported on joists. To keep the joists and the flooring dry, some kind of underfloor ventilation is essential. This takes the form of airbricks in the outer walls.

The first thing to check is that all the existing airbricks are free of debris and have not been blocked up in the mistaken belief that this will save money on heating. Next, check that there are enough airbricks – there should be one airbrick for every 2m (6ft) of wall length. Inserting a new airbrick is not difficult, as most match the size of standard bricks.

Decide where you want to put it, drill out the mortar around the existing brick and remove it. With a cavity wall, you will have to continue the hole through the inner wall and fit a terracotta liner to maintain the airflow. Use the corners of the hole in the outer wall to line up and drill four holes in the inner wall, then chip out the hole with a bolster (stonecutter's) chisel and club (spalling) hammer, working from the inside. You will need to lift floorboards to do this.

Fit the airbrick from the outside, applying mortar to the bottom of the hole and the top of the brick, pushing mortar in the sides. Point the mortar joints to the same profile as the surrounding joints. Mortar the liner in place from inside the house.

VENTILATING ROOF SPACES

If your house has a gable end wall, the roof space can be ventilated by fitting airbricks in the gable. If the house is semi-detached, ask your neighbour to do the same, and fit another airbrick in the party wall to allow air to circulate.

SAFE VENTILATION

There are two very important points to remember concerning ventilation. Firstly, many fuel-burning appliances need an adequate supply of fresh air to work efficiently and safely, so rooms where they are sited must contain provision for this if they are well sealed against natural draughts. Secondly, disused flues must be ventilated at top and bottom; if they are not, condensation can occur within the flue, which may show up as damp patches on the internal chimney walls.

TIP

You may need to install more airbricks in a room where there is a solid concrete hearth (from an old cooking range, say). This can create "dead" areas which may need extra ventilation to prevent rot.

1 Airbricks are the same size as one, two or three bricks. To fit one, start by drilling a series of closely-spaced holes through the joint around a brick.

2 Then use the club (spalling) hammer and a wide bolster (stonecutter's) chisel to cut out the brickwork. With solid walls, drill holes right through and work from inside too.

3 Fit a cavity liner through to the inner wall if the wall is of cavity construction, then trowel a bed of fairly wet mortar on to the bottom of the opening.

4 Butter mortar on to the top of the airbrick and slide in place. Push more mortar into the gaps at the sides. Inside, make good the wall with plaster and cover the opening with a ventilator grille.

5 As an alternative to the traditional terracotta airbrick, fit a two-part plastic version. The sleeves interlock to line the hole as the two parts are pushed together.

6 Slide the outer section into place, and point around it. Slide the inner section into place from the inside of the house. Make good the plaster and fit its cover grille.

OVERCOMING DAMP CONDITIONS

Damp conditions can cause serious problems if allowed to persist in the home, even leading to structural decay, so it is essential to deal with damp as soon as it becomes obvious. The first task is to recognize the type of damp you are faced with: it could be condensation, caused by moisture inside the home, or penetrating or rising damp from outside. In some cases, finding a remedy is relatively straightforward; in others, solving the problem can be complex and costly, and may require the involvement of professionals. If damp conditions are not corrected, they may lead to wet rot or dry rot in structural wooden framing. Both can be a major problem if not tackled quickly, since they weaken the wood with potentially disastrous consequences.

DAMP

This can ruin decorations, destroy floorcoverings, damage walls and plaster, and cause woodwork to rot, so it is important not only to treat the symptoms, but also to track down the causes. These might be rain coming in through the roof or walls, condensation, moisture being absorbed from the ground, or a combination of any of these.

PENETRATING DAMP

This is caused by moisture getting in from the outside, often because of wear and tear to the structure of your home, but it may also affect solid walls that are subjected to strong driving rain. The first sign of penetrating damp appears after a heavy downpour and can occur almost anywhere, although it may be some distance from the actual leak; mould often forms directly behind where the problem lies. Pay particular attention to rainwater systems, which are common causes of penetrating damp.

RISING DAMP

This is caused by water soaking up through floors and walls, and is usually confined to a 1m (3ft) band above ground level. It is a constant problem, even during dry spells.

The main areas to check for rising damp are the damp-proof course (DPC) around the foot of walls, and damp-proof membrane (DPM) in the ground floor. Older properties were often built without either, which can lead to widespread rising damp. If existing

ABOVE: A patch of mould on the inner face of an external wall is usually the first sign of penetrating damp.

ABOVE: Gaps between masonry and woodwork around windows will let in rain, causing patches of damp to occur.

materials have broken down or structural movement has caused defects, there may be isolated, but spreading, patches of damp where water is penetrating. A DPC that is less than 150mm (6in) above ground level will allow rain to splash above it and penetrate the wall, which may cause damp patches at skirting (baseboard) level. If a DPC has been bridged, there will be evidence of damp just above skirting level. A wall cavity filled with rubble may also allow damp to penetrate.

DEALING WITH DAMP

Once the cause of penetrating damp has been traced and repaired, the problem will be eradicated. When the damp patches have dried out, it may be necessary to replaster those areas and make good any decorations.

Dealing with a DPC that has been bridged is quite straightforward. If the ground level is the cause, digging a 150mm (6in) trench along the house wall, then filling it with gravel will allow rainwater to drain away rapidly. When you suspect that debris in the cavity is the cause, removing a few bricks will give access to remove it.

The remedy for rising damp caused by a non-existent or defective DPC or DPM is not so easy; the only solution is to install a replacement or make repairs.

DAMP-PROOFING METHODS

Laying a new damp-proof membrane involves digging up and re-laying the floor slab, which is the most effective method of damp-proofing a concrete floor. However, a floor can also be damp-proofed by applying several coats of moisture-curing urethane, but it is essential that any leaky patches are sealed first with a hydraulic cement.

A third option is to apply two coats of rubberized bitumen emulsion to the old surface, then cover this with a cement/sand screed, which will raise the level of the floor by about 50mm (2in).

Whichever method you choose, the DPM material should be taken up the adjoining walls to meet the DPC, if there is one. The problem of damp floors caused by rising ground-water levels, which typically affects basements, is more serious and requires structural waterproofing or "tanking". This is certainly a job for the professionals.

ABOVE: A damp-proof course should be clear of soil, debris or plants growing up walls, otherwise moisture can bypass it.

INSTALLING A DAMP-PROOF COURSE

There are many ways of installing a damp-proof course, ranging from physical DPCs that are cut into the brickwork to chemical slurries, which are pumped into a series of drilled holes.

In theory, it is possible to do the job yourself, but dealing with rising damp is rarely simple; it is worth seeking the advice of professionals. If there is a mortgage on your home, the lender may require a guarantee of workmanship, which rules out tackling the job yourself. The standard of workmanship is as important as the system used, so choosing a reputable company that offers an insurance-backed guarantee is essential, and often compulsory.

If you do choose to go ahead yourself, you should be able to hire the necessary equipment to install a chemical DPC, and the same company may supply the chemical too.

After installing a DPC, walls and floors can take up to a month for each 25mm (1in) to dry out, while old plaster may be heavily contaminated with salts from rising damp, which will continue to absorb moisture from the air. Delay replastering for as long as possible to allow the walls to dry out.

1 A chemical damp-proof course is injected into a line of holes drilled in the wall about 115mm (4½in) apart.

2 Once injected into the drilled holes, the chemicals overlap to form a continuous impermeable barrier.

3 When the fluid is dry, the drilled holes are filled with mortar and then a rendered surface can be painted.

WATERPROOFING WALLS

The external walls of modern brick houses are built with a cavity between the inner and outer leaves of the wall that effectively prevents damp from reaching the inner leaf. Unless the cavity becomes bridged in some way, there should be no problems with penetrating damp. However, older properties are likely to have been built with solid walls and it is possible that, over time, the masonry may become porous, allowing damp to penetrate to the inside.

Penetrating damp in solid walls is difficult to cure, and one solution, albeit rather drastic, is to build false walls inside, complete with vapour barriers, effectively creating cavity walls. However, this solution is expensive, and it will reduce the size of rooms considerably.

Less expensive is to treat the outer faces of the walls with a water-repellent coating. This will prevent rainwater from soaking into the walls and reaching the interior.

The first job is to clean the walls and make good any structural defects. Wash them down and treat them with a fungicide to kill off any mould. Check the condition of the mortar joints and repoint any that are soft and crumbling; fill cracks in the joints or bricks with mortar or an exterior-grade filler.

When the walls have dried, brush on the water-repellent liquid, following the manufacturer's instructions; you may need to apply more than one coat.

1 Brush, clean, and remove any fungal growth from the wall. Fill any surface cracks so that the surface is sound.

2 Apply the water seal by brush, working from the bottom up, coating the whole wall. If necessary, apply a second coat.

CONDENSATION

When warm, moist air reaches a cold surface, such as a wall exposed to icy winter winds or ceramic tiles, the result is condensation. It is most likely to occur in bathrooms and kitchens where the main activities are bathing, washing and cooking.

Controlling condensation requires a fine balance between good ventilation and adequate heating, but while the modern home is warm, it is also well insulated and draughtproofed, so the level of ventilation is often poor. The key to success is to provide sufficient ventilation, without allowing expensive heat to escape.

Ventilation can be provided by a variety of passive and active means. Passive ventilation may be achieved by opening windows and/or fitting airbricks and simple vents. Active ventilation relies on powered extractor fans.

CONDENSATION OR DAMP?

If you are not sure if a moisture problem is due to condensation or damp, lay a piece of aluminium foil over the patch, seal the edges with adhesive tape and leave it for 48 hours. Condensation will cause beads of moisture to appear on the surface of the foil; penetrating or rising damp will produce beads of moisture underneath the foil.

ABOVE: Water vapour from everyday activities, such as cooking, can cause condensation.

ABOVE: Poor ventilation will make condensation problems worse.

COPING WITH CONDENSATION

Steam from cooking can be removed by a fully vented cooker hood, but where a great deal of steam is produced, when you take a shower for example, the best way to remove it from the room is with an extractor fan.

To be quick and efficient, the fan must be sited properly and it should be the correct size for the room. In a kitchen, a fan must be capable of ten to 15 air changes per hour, and in bathrooms six to eight air changes per hour, which should be increased to 15 to 20 air changes for a power shower. Simply multiply the volume of the room by the number of air changes required and look for a fan that offers the same cubic metre/foot capacity per hour (m³/hr or ft³/hr).

An extractor fan should be installed as high as possible on the wall, and as far as possible from the main source

of ventilation; usually diagonally opposite the main door is ideal.

More widespread condensation can be alleviated with an electric dehumidifier, which draws air from the room, passes it over cold coils to condense it, then collects the drips of water. The dry air is then drawn over heated coils and released back into the room as heat.

TIPS

• In bathrooms, keep the door shut when taking a bath. When running a bath, run the cold water first to minimize the amount of steam that is produced.
• Where condensation occurs in a confined space, such as a built-in wardrobe, causing mould and mildew, use silica gel crystals to absorb excess moisture from the air.
• In kitchens, make sure a tumble-drier is properly vented.

RIGHT: A cooker hood removes steam from cooking at source. Beware, however, since some cooker hoods merely recirculate the air, filtering out the particles from cooking, but not the moisture. For this, you must have an extractor hood. Remember, too, that kettles produce steam, as do other forms of cooking that may not be in range of a cooker hood. Consequently, it may be worth adding a window vent or even an additional extractor fan.

DRY ROT

The fungus that causes dry rot loves moist, humid conditions and has a taste for resins and silicones in untreated wood. However, the grey strands are fine enough to penetrate masonry, which means that it can spread rapidly from room to room.

Untreated dry rot will destroy floors, doors and skirtings (baseboards), and infect plaster and ceilings. Initially, it manifests itself as a brownish-red dust, but within days the spores will have developed into a fungus that looks like a mushroom growing upside-down, and it also gives off a distinctive musty smell. This is the final stage of germination, by which time the fungus will be producing millions of spores to infect surrounding areas.

Dealing with dry rot is a job that should be entrusted to a specialist, as it may recur if not treated properly. Make sure you choose a reputable company that offers an insurance-backed guarantee.

PREVENTATIVE ACTION

• Make sure that a damp-proof course (DPC) has not been bridged, by looking for tell-tale signs of damp on walls above skirtings (baseboards).

• Dry rot will not flourish in well-ventilated areas, so make sure there is good ventilation in roofs and under suspended wooden floors. If necessary, fit air vents or extractor fans in soffits and gable end walls.

ABOVE: An example of severe dry rot on a destroyed wooden floor.

ABOVE: A sporophore, or dry rot fungus, on a structural roof timber. Immediate action is necessary as soon as the fungus is spotted to minimize its spread through wooden structures.

ABOVE: Inspect your loft (attic) space and check for the first signs of dry rot. Ensure there is good ventilation in the loft and under the floors to help prevent the conditions in which dry rot can flourish.

WET ROT

This thrives on wet wood and frequently appears where wood is close to the ground or near leaking plumbing, and in woodwork where the protective paint coating has broken down. Skirtings (baseboards) may also be affected where a damp-proof course is defective.

Wet rot can be due to a number of species of fungus, but the most common consist of brown or black strands that appear on the surface, causing the wood to crack and eventually disintegrate. Affected wood tends to look darker than healthy wood and feels spongy.

Once the cause of the damp conditions that have led to the problem is eliminated, wet rot fungus will die. Treat small areas, such as window frames, with proprietary wood hardener solution and insert preservative tablets into holes drilled into the wood to stop any recurrence. Where damage is extensive, the wood should be cut out and replaced.

REPAIRING WET ROT

1 Chisel out all the rotten wood, making sure only sound wood is left.

2 Brush the sound wood with hardener and leave to dry as recommended.

3 To fit wood preservative sticks, drill holes of the correct size in the sound wood. Push the preservative sticks into the drilled holes and below the surface.

4 Fill the damaged area with exterior wood filler. Leave to dry before sanding. Then apply a good paint finish.

INDEX

The publisher would like to thank
the following for supplying pictures:
D.I.Y. Photo Library 8bl, 58t, br;
Simon J. Gilham 57, 61; HSS Hire
Tools 54b, 58bl; Rentokil 54tl, 62t,
bl, br; Thompson's (Ronseal Ltd.,
Thorncliff Park, Chapeltown, Sheffield
S35 2YP, England; tel. (0114) 246
7171; website www.ronseal.co.uk)
1tl, 5bm, 54tr, 59bl, br.